The Virgo Personality

*Understanding Your Own
Innate Virgo Personality Traits
and Virgo Characteristics to
Become a Better Virgo Woman*

by Analise Zanardi

Table of Contents

Introduction

If you were born from August 23 to September 22, then you are a Virgo. If that means nothing to you besides a tiny paragraph in a newspaper or a magazine, then you've got a lot more to learn about astrology - so let's start there.

Astrology is not about predestination, nor is it about fortune telling. It simply states that at the moment of your birth, the sun, moon, stars, planets, and constellations were arranged in such a way that you became predisposed to certain personality traits. Depending on what these are, you have certain ingrained strengths and weaknesses.

Astrology does not ignore the effects of your individual upbringing, your environment, nor your personal experiences. Neither does it claim to be able to map out your future as if your life were a pre-written book with an immutable beginning, middle, and end.

What it does claim is that the heavens played a role in shaping your mental landscape. Everything you experienced from the moment you entered this world, therefore, will be filtered and understood through that personal landscape. Think of an astrology chart as map of that personal landscape, a tool that helps you better understand yourself.

This isn't psychoanalysis. Freud's obsession with penile envy and vaginal terror reveals more about his personal psychosis than it does about people — which is why most reputable psychological associations today consider it to be utter nonsense.

The only reason psychoanalysis still exists (albeit in forms that Freud would no longer recognize) is that we have a mountain of scientific evidence proving that he got two things right.

The first is that what goes on in our heads has an effect on how we view the world around us, how we interpret that information, and how we react based on that information. Second, much of our personalities are shaped by what happens to us early in life.

This is pretty much what the ancient astrologers said. They took it a step further, however, by saying that the heavenly bodies also play a role.

Socrates once claimed that "an unexamined life is not worth living." It makes sense if you think about it. People have a choice: to live on automatic mode based on instincts and circumstance, or to live consciously with an understanding of themselves.

The former live like animals, are reactive, and simply go with the flow — like sheep. The latter become empowered, tend to think before they act, and are therefore proactive.

So, Virgo woman, which kind of life would you prefer to live?

Chapter 1: Understanding Astrology

Astrology comes from two Greek words: "astro" and "logos." These mean "stars" and "language, respectively. We can therefore understand this word to mean "the language of the stars."

To understand this language, you have to first look up, preferably at night so you can actually see those stars. You know about the Big Dipper and Orion, but did you know that all twelve signs of the zodiac are also constellations? Different cultures have drawn their own constellations, but here in the West, we recognize 88 of them.

Our planet orbits the sun, but from our point of view, it's the sun that does the orbiting. The path that the sun takes across the sky is called the plane of the ecliptic. In fact, all the planets in our solar system also travel across this plane, which is what makes astrology charts possible.

Of the 88 constellations, thirteen lie on the plane of the ecliptic, but only twelve are used. Why? Well, from our point of view, the plane of the ecliptic is a circle — like a belt or a wide ring around our sky. A circle is made up of 360°, so it's easier to divide 360 by 12 instead of 13. In doing this, we split our sky up into twelve equal segments of 30° each.

As the sun moves across the sky, each of these twelve constellations provides a backdrop for it. Since the constellations come in different shapes and sizes, the sun can't possibly spend the same amount of time travelling through each of them. It spends 45 days in Virgo, for example, but only seven days in Scorpio.

To deal with this problem, Ophiuchus, the thirteenth constellation, got dumped. Doing this allowed the ancient astrologers to assign uniform times to all the twelve signs of the zodiac.

In case you were wondering, Ophiuchus represents a man holding a snake, and stands opposite Orion. If we included it in astrology, we would put it between Sagittarius and Scorpio. If you're in the northern part of the planet, you can best see it in summer

At the time you were born, the sun was making its journey across the constellation of Virgo. It did this by first exiting Libra, and when it leaves your sign, it'll go into Leo. Depending on how close or how far it is from the other signs when you were born, certain other characteristics sort of "bleed" into yours, which also has an effect on you.

Chapter 2: Am I Really a Virgo?

The astrology that the West practices today came from the ancient Babylonians (now part of modern day Iraq) who lived some 3,000 years ago. While later cultures (like the Greeks) added their own input over the millennium, the methodology we still use today is based on the original Babylonian model.

In 2010, however, astronomers from the Minnesota Planetarium Society claimed that we've all been going about it wrong. Our planet's axis has changed over the millennium and will continue to do so — it's what planets do, apparently, a process called axial tilt.

What this means is that the North Pole isn't always where it's been, nor will it always stay where it currently is. In the 3,000 years since the Babylonians came up with astrology, the zodiac has moved up by about a month. As such, we've all been plotting the sun's path across the twelve signs of the zodiac incorrectly (though recently, some astrologers have been including Ophiuchus).

Leaving the geeky stuff behind, what this means is that the sign you think you were born under is not actually the sign you should have been born under. Did that go over your head?

According to the Minnesota astronomers, the following is a more accurate and updated way to determine your astrological sign:

Capricorn: Jan 20 - Feb 16   **Aquarius:** Feb 16 - March 11

Pisces: March 11 – April 18   **Aries**: April 18 – May 13

Taurus: May 13 – June 21   **Gemini**: June 21 – July 20

Cancer: July 20 – Aug 10   **Leo:** Aug 10 – Sept 16

Virgo: Sept 16 – Oct 30   **Libra:** Oct 30 – Nov 23

Scorpio: Nov 23 – 29   **Ophiuchus**: Nov 29 – Dec 17

Sagittarius: Dec 17 – Jan 20

There's only one problem with this. The astrology that the West has been practicing since the 2nd century has also changed.

Western astrology is strictly based on the tropical zodiac which is fixed to the seasons and aligned to the equinoctial points — which means it doesn't change. The sidereal zodiac used in the East is fixed upon the constellations — which is the one that should indeed change.

What this means for you is that if your horoscope is based on the Western tropical zodiac (and if you're an American or European, then it probably is), then don't panic. You're still a Virgo!

Assuming you still want to think of yourself as a Virgo, then let's continue.

Chapter 3: Symbology of Virgo

Virgo is the Latin word for virgin (regardless of gender), but it's also related to the word "virga," which means "young shoot," for a plant. In common usage, however, virgo was also used to mean "self-contained," which is pretty much the dominant characteristic of those born under this sign.

If you do a Google image search of this constellation, you'll understand why this sign generally depicts a woman reclining, as if on a couch (like upper class Romans did at meals). As with upper class Roman women, Virgos tend to be fastidious in their appearance and manners, as well as generally shy and reserved.

Because of this, they sometimes come across as being hard-to-get, at best, or snobbish, at worst. This is not necessarily true, but they just can't help giving off those "keep your distance, or else" vibes.

As a result, some Virgo women wonder why, despite their beauty, others get approached but not them. Still others know that they're giving off those "back off, I mean it" signals, but can't stop themselves from doing so because they honestly don't know how to.

The classical depiction of Virgo is based on Astraea (Star Maiden) who was associated with the goddess of justice, Dike (pronounced *dee-kee*, not *daik* — but yes, she's where we get that derogatory term for "lesbian" from). In Greek mythology, Astraea was the last of the gods to abandon the earth when the Silver Age ended and ushered in the violent and sinful Iron Age (the current one we're living in).

For this reason, Virgos are also associated with fidelity and the earth. When the going gets rough, Virgo women are usually the last to get going. While a noble sentiment and practice, this isn't always a good thing — especially when it comes to abusive relationships, dead end jobs, and hopeless situations. As a result, Virgo women are also renowned for stubbornness.

The classical image of Virgo usually depicts a woman holding a sheaf or a bundle of wheat. This represents wisdom, experience, and wealth. It also shows that she is indeed a self-contained woman. In other words, this is not the kind of girl who depends on others for a meal.

That wheat bundle also defines another aspect of the Virgo woman. Since Virgo women have a strong independent streak and don't open up to others so easily, they are deathly terrified of being dependent on others. This results in three major characteristics.

The first is that Virgo women tend to be very ambitious and materialistic. It isn't the money and the bling-bling they're after, per se. It's the sense of security, independence, and power that money brings.

Second, Virgos have a great deal of respect for order and rank. Law, tradition, custom, and hierarchies provide the security they crave. These things, while stifling for some, create the type of world which Virgos thrive in. There's no point in keeping people at bay and in making money if there were no institutions in place to enforce one's will and protect one's property, after all.

Finally, Virgos are very analytical — a requirement for successful agricultural production. They dislike chaos, so they approach things in an orderly fashion. This can be seen in the care they take with their appearance and behavior, their sense of aesthetics, and in the methodical way they work.

Methodical is another key word to understanding Virgos. The twelve signs are each associated with an element, and as mentioned earlier, Virgo belongs to that of earth.

Perhaps Virgo woman's strength is also her weakness. The astrological symbol for this sign is ♍, which depicts an "M" with a sort of loop at the end. The two arches of the symbol represent the wings that sometimes grace depictions of Virgo.

This means that she's not an ordinary woman, but one who stands on an elevated position above everyone else. Virgo woman's natural reserve has people putting her on a pedestal, but as the old saying goes: "it gets very lonely at the top."

And since it's lonely at the top, Virgo women can become isolated and out of touch. This results in some of them becoming jaded, sceptical, cold, detached, inflexible, and interfering. It is not uncommon, therefore, for Virgo women to have relationship problems, if they even have them at all.

As to the loop at the end of the ♍, well that's where it gets downright sexist and complicated. Most believe it represents a woman's crossed legs. In other words, it means "DO NOT ENTER," which is why Virgo means virgin. Get it? Others suggest it means the self-contained nature that this sign represents.

That loop, however, opens up into two tails — like a pair of spread legs. In other words, Virgo's natural reserve is something of a sham. Behind that protective wall is a passionate woman who has such a great capacity for love that she's very picky about who to give it to.

Virgo women are therefore generally conflicted about everything. Openly reserved, but inwardly passionate; analytical and logical, but emotionally hungry; ambitious, but respects hierarchies. Little wonder, then, that you're reading this, huh? Poor thing...

Chapter 4: Fine Tuning Your Sign

Since there were many astrological factors that had an effect on your personality at the moment you were born, it would be surprising if you were able to relate to literally everything cited in the previous chapter. There are Virgos, for example, who are messy, loud-mouthed, in-your-face slobs. So how did this happen?

Remember how the introduction explained the value of your internal mental landscape? Remember, too, how a sign's proximity to others has an effect on how that internal landscape is formed? And finally, remember how it explained that the sun does not really spend an equal amount of time in each zodiac sign?

Wonderful! So before you despair and sue the hospital for getting your birth certificate wrong, let's do a little more fine-tuning so you can get the most out of your sign.

The best way to do this is by getting an astrologer to create a personalized natal chart of the exact time, date, and place of your birth. Barring that, there's a few more things to consider.

Although Virgo usually covers August 23 to September 22, it's actually a lot more complicated than that. This is why they come up with new books every year. They need to update the information based on the astronomical data that comes into play for that year.

The sun actually enters Virgo at around August 21, but the effects don't become immediately apparent for several more days. Usually, Virgo comes into its full power at around August 29 and continues at full strength till around September 20. After that, its influence begins to wane for another seven days till the influence of the next sign (which is Libra) starts to really exert itself.

Although we divide the plane of the ecliptic into twelve neat divisions, each composed of 30°, the effects of each sign are not always so clear cut. The official division between each sign is called a cusp (Latin for "spear" or "point"), but they were set merely for convenience and to ensure uniformity. This is why the sun can straddle a cusp, or put another way, straddle two signs at the same time.

This is why each sign is split into three decans, the Latin word for "ten." So 1° to 10° is closer to the previous sign of Leo and is called the 1st decan; 11° to 20° is the second decan and is when the typical Virgo characteristics are at their height; while 21° to 30° is the third decan and where we begin to see traits from Libra start to bleed in.

Astrologers agree (even those who use the sidereal zodiac) that there are generally eight types of Virgos:

1) There's the workaholic and messy type who loves tools and tends to be a tech geek, the type that guys like to hang around with as they mess about in their garage or on their computers,

2) There's the intellectual type who lives in her head and can't be bothered to eat regularly, dress neatly, comb her hair, or clean her house and car,

3) There's the care-giving Mother Theresa type who'll go off into war zones to help both sides, or be willing to adopt more children than Angelina Jolie,

4) There's the arts-and-crafts type who seems to always have paint or glue on her fingers and hair, so don't even get started on her house or work space,

5) There's the ritualistic type who just has to do everything at the right time and in the exact order, or else she falls apart,

6) There's the art and literary critic. This Virgo is the kind who has many genuine admirers but few real friends because she just can't stop being an art and literary critic,

7) There's the facts-and-figures archivist-librarian type who remembers everything, including how you forgot

to give her a gift on her birthday eleven years ago even though she gave you one every year, and finally,

8) There's the Virgo who's more Leo or Libra to really be in the Virgo club.

There is not enough time in the day to discuss all the factors which affect a person's mental landscape and external habits, but we can explore some of the more major ones.

Chapter 5: The Three Decans

Each decan makes up roughly ten days. During this period, however, it's not just the sun which cruises through Virgo. The other planets also zoom by, further adding their own unique influence to this sign. To make things even more wonderfully complicated, the moon also has to have its say, but that's already getting too technical for our purposes.

The planet which dominates Virgo is Mercury. Mercury was the messenger god of the Roman pantheon, whose Greek persona was Hermes. Whatever you choose to call him, he was responsible for carrying prayers to the gods and sending back their reply (if any), the one who helped the dead move into the afterlife, and is associated with cunning, wit, and the intellect.

Although this planet holds the most influence over Virgo, its power over those born under this sign is not absolute. As the sun passes through this constellation, Mercury's influence is shared, modified, or even mitigated by the other planets which pass by for a brief visit.

First Decan: August 23 to September 1

Mercury's influence is strongest at this time, so those born during this period are natural communicators — masters of the written and spoken word. These women make great writers, teachers, speakers, lecturers, lawyers, diplomats, and sales reps.

Unfortunately, they also make great scam artists, liars, and manipulators. While generally intelligent, there is a tendency for first decans to try to come across as being more intelligent, capable, or profound than they really are. This is again due to Mercury, who is also the god of thieves, liars, and poets; though not necessarily in that order.

Since Virgo is the sixth, and therefore the most balanced of the twelve signs, there is also a tendency to play peace keeper. While a noble sentiment, this role also requires control. If not tempered, first decan women become overly controlling, too obsessive about cleanliness and order, and can become interfering.

Ever seen statues or pictures of that naked guy with wings on his feet, holding a staff with serpents on it? That's Mercury again, who's also associated with healing. This is explains why first decans are often attracted to the healing arts and why many tend to be health-conscious.

The downside, however, is when they become hypochondriacs. Some Virgos become obsessed with alternative medicine, becoming experts in arcane cures, and have the perfect health advice for everyone — even those who are tired of hearing it.

First decan types are incredibly adaptable and quite a few are either left-handed or ambidextrous. Hard-working and ambitious, they enjoy being busy, but sometimes become workaholics at the expense of their relationships and health. While not above manual labor, these types prefer using their heads.

Second Decan: September 2 to September 11

Saturn was the Roman god of wealth, agriculture, time, and dissolution. His feast day, the Saturnalia, was celebrated with banquets and gifts, and is where we got the word "Saturday" from. Since he's also a serious god associated with important lessons, this is also where we got the word "saturnine" from. Saturn rules this decan and therefore explains a lot.

Those born during this decan are natural organizers, have indomitable will, and are generally unflappable; perfect examples of the British stiff upper lip stereotype. Second decan women tend to be heavy set and very solid, work horses who don't seem to understand the word "no" — sometimes at the expense of their own health. Dry skin also tends to be a problem, requiring a regimen of moisturizers.

These people make great employees, so long as there's room for growth and promotion. If so, then those above have ample reason to be nervous. If her workplace offers none of these, then she won't stay for long. Unfortunately, this can result in a lot of job hopping with a long resume of short-term jobs that impresses no one.

Women born at this time are obsessed with success, recognition, and awards. They are highly competitive, sometimes to the point of ruthlessness. Once they reach a higher station, however, they tend to be protective over those beneath them. Virgo women generally make good bosses — great at being tactful, at delegation, and at motivating staff.

They are perfectionists, however, and expect the same of others, both those above and beneath them. This can lead to impatience, at times, as well as to misunderstanding and conflicts with both superiors and underlings.

Unfortunately, the second decan of Virgo also comes with a Capricorn sub-influence. Never mind what that is. All you need to know is that this can create obstacles in a second decan woman's life and/or career, turning her into a late bloomer.

This means that no matter how hard they work, it's unlikely that they'll achieve any real financial success till sometime in their 30s. Once they reach this period, things may start to pick up, but it's unlikely that they'll reach the pinnacle till their late 50s, or thereabouts.

This is a particularly dangerous time. While they begin to see evidence of their hard work finally paying off, the fact that it'll rarely fall into their laps because of so many obstacles can make them bitter, cynical, and confrontational. There is even the possibility that long bouts of depression and extreme self-doubt can hit, which can have a negative impact on those around them, especially family and friends.

The best way to deal with this is to understand that there's only so much one can do. Capricorn's influence has a way of making things go awry, but if one can continue to plod through (an inherent talent of Virgos), there will be rewards in the end.

Third Decan: September 12 to September 23

This is ruled by Venus, the goddess of love. It does, however, also come with a Taurus sub-influence, generating some very interesting results.

The Venus influence produces women who are quiet, reserved, shy, timid, and very uncomfortable with attention. This is a pity, because they generally have fine skin texture, well-proportioned bodies, sensual lips, as well as pleasant singing and speaking voices.

They also tend to be gifted with a good ear for pitch, making music an ideal profession. Those who do work in music tend to take back-up or chorus roles — anything to ensure that they're not in the limelight. While they love nice clothes and accessories, they like to keep things simple and toned down, not loud and garish.

They can be easily moved by emotions, falling in love quickly and getting hurt just as quickly. It isn't often easy to tell, however, because of their talent for bottling things up. These women are not wimps, though. They have an amazing degree of patience and can take a lot of criticism, pressure, and disappointment. But it can go too far, especially in abusive relationships.

Fortunately they have limits, which is where the Taurus sub-influence comes in. Bulls are not as temperamental as they are often depicted. In fact, they usually have to be goaded into entering the bull-fighting ring.

While Venus is sensitive and patient, Taurus has a steely strength and an explosive temper. Pushed too far, third decan women can snap back, surprising not just themselves, but others, as well. As such, these women can often be passive aggressive, using silence and stubbornness as weapons, till they finally explode.

Though women born under this decan can be flexible, they much prefer routine. While not generally ambitious, they can be frighteningly persistent when they set their minds on something. Combined with their stubbornness, persistence, methodical nature, and people's tendency to underestimate them (including themselves), they can go very far.

Chapter 6: The Cusps

The sun's straddling of two signs is responsible for those who feel they don't typify their sign. So let's shed light on these personality types.

Leo-Virgo Cusp: August 19 to August 24

Leo's roaring flamboyance contrasts with Virgo's bashfulness, and results in raging extroverts who go through bouts of serious alone-time. These are excellent communicators who have great conversational and manipulative skills, making them excellent lawyers, diplomats, salespeople, and televangelists.

They also love to gamble. Combined with their natural sociability, decisiveness, stubbornness, persistence, attention to detail, and quick wit, they usually make good business people — provided they can temper their fascination with risk.

Leo-Virgo cusp women are generally athletic, obsessed with health, and fastidious about nutrition and hygiene. They generally enjoy group sports over solitary ones like jogging, and are great at managing teams — another plus for those interested in business. A downside is that they can get too hung up over their personal appearance, becoming vain and shallow, like gym bunnies and fashion victims.

Leo's influence can make them very confrontational and domineering, however, while Virgo's can make them overly critical and secretive. These women will bully men into dates, then treat them like job applicants during that date. Those they do love will rarely hear that word, however. These women are suspicious of words, preferring show over tell.

Virgo-Libra Cusp: September 19 to September 24

Women born at this time are obsessed with beauty. They love the arts, attractive people, and make great art collectors and museum curators. They're not the flighty types, however. Virgo's influence keeps them down-to-earth with a keen eye for details and a strong obsession with organization.

A weakness of this type, however, is that while they appreciate beauty and talent, they can lack imagination. They can tell you why a piece of art is great, but can rarely create one, themselves. They are also health conscious, but there is the danger of becoming hypochondriacs.

This love of beauty can also make them vain, shallow, compulsive, and obsessive about fashion and appearances. For those with shallow pockets, this can be troublesome. Virgo-Libra cusp women can also be very nit-picky, seeing flaws in everything, including themselves. This is the type who pressures her children into getting straight As, and demands that they become doctors, lawyers, and engineers — constantly reminding them of the painful hours she spent in labor.

Overall, however, these women are generally sociable, kind and patient, romantic, devoted, and playful. Libra's influence also makes them open-minded and scrupulously fair, making them great diplomats and judges. They love conversation, are excellent at debates, and have a talent for playing the devil's advocate — which can sometimes be frustrating to their family, friends, and lovers.

Chapter 7: General Advice

Being a Virgo is not easy, and giving generic advice to a sign that includes so many permutations is not possible. That said, there are certain threads that run through all types of Virgo women. If taken with a grain of salt and adapted according to your specific situation, the following can go a long way.

You are your own obstacle

Life is hard enough, but when you have an elevated, celestial virgin telling you to hold back, it can get even harder. Your sign makes you rigid, which is why your element is earth. This is why you tend to put duty and obligation over your own personal happiness, and your career or routine over your personal life.

The world is not black and white

Never mind that you were raised to believe otherwise. The world isn't perfect and no matter what you do, it never will be. It is the very imperfection and unpredictability of the world that makes it an exciting place to live in, but you have to be able to accept it as it is, not as you want it to be.

It is not wrong to judge or to criticize — we are all entitled to our opinions. But don't let that keep you from engaging with different people or pursuing interests just because society disapproves. You have a right to be odd, strange, or different if you want to be.

Step up

It is a well-known fact that Virgo women often stay in jobs or positions they are over-qualified for. This is because of their obsession with appearances, perfectionism, and order. Even if you know you're qualified for a senior level position, you're afraid you might fail and everyone will know. So you settle for the junior level position, instead, since it makes you look perfect.

In relationships, Virgo women tend to remain with men (or other women), even when there's no spark in it. This is because they like routine, are afraid of what others will think, or because they fear there might not be anyone else out there for them. Unless you understand that happiness rests with you and with the choices you make, not in other people, your life will continue to be dull.

Whether in their jobs or in their personal lives, Virgo women tend to wait for the perfect moment. This falls in line with their idea of a structured, hierarchical world; that if they work hard enough and persist long enough, the right time will fall in their laps.

It will never happen. This is why a common complaint of Virgo women is that they feel they're not living their lives to the fullest.

As a Virgo, you are trapped between virginal restraint and mercurial temperament. Let the former keep you safe, grounded, and secure; but let the latter guide and inspire you to act.

Finally, I'd like to thank you for purchasing this book! If you enjoyed it or found it helpful, I'd greatly appreciate it if you'd take a moment to leave a review on Amazon. Thank you!

FREE BONUS!

Visit www.attractandcaptivate.com/bonus to claim this free
exclusive bonus content now.

37747525R00029

Made in the USA
San Bernardino, CA
25 August 2016